Con

C000007781

Walk
1. The 3 Village Round
2. The Tissington Round
3. The Waterwheel Walk
4. The Manifold Way Circular   5   8   2.0
5. Yerley Hill Round   5.3   8.5   2-3
6. The Tissington to Fenny Bentley Trail   5.3   8.6   3
7. Ilam to Calton Round   5.6   9   2-3
8. Clifton & Compton Circular   5.9   9.5   4
9. Dove Dale, Wood & River Walk   7   11.3   3

Walking times shown are approximate and depend on fitness, weight of rucksack, weather, conditions underfoot and height climbed.

Level of Difficulty 1 = Easy, 3 = Moderate, 6 = Hard
Walks 1,2,4,6,9 and part of 7 are shown on O.S. Explorer maps No. OL24 The Peak District – White Peak Area, & walks 3,5,8 and part of 7 are shown on Explorer No. 259 Derby,

Every effort has been made to ascertain the accuracy of the walks described. The description of a route or track is not necessarily a right of way.

Some abbreviations have been used in the text to shorten it and make it more concise: -
PF = Public Footpath   RT = Right   LT = Left   FB = Footbridge
CP = Car Park   m = metres   km = kilometres   °M = magnetic
RD = Road   BW = Bridleway

Walkers are strongly advised to have the appropriate clothing and footwear for these walks.
• Boots/walking shoes.
• Waterproof Jacket.
• Over trousers.
• Small Rucksack for food, drinks and spare clothing.
• Hat & Gloves.
• Compass & map.

ISBN 978-1-903568-50-7

Walk 1 The 3 Village Round   **Distance** 4.3 miles/6 km
Start GR. 130555 Start in Alstonefield by the telephone box.
Walk Time 2 hrs 5 mins
Terrain A pleasant walk over many fields with only a few hills. There are two pubs for refreshment, one in Wetton and one in Alstonefield.

From the telephone box in Alstonefield, walk across to the Alstonefield Memorial Hall and turn LT by the sign for Wetton, then immediately LT again by the side of the houses onto a track (1).

At a BW sign for Stanshope, continue straight ahead by the opening at the farm gate. Walk straight down the field. At the bottom, walk between the two walls as you descend slightly.

Go through a gate and descend to the bottom of the ravine in Milldale (2). Cross the minor RD there and ascend the far side, following the PF sign to Stanshope. You pass Grove Farm on your LT then come on to the minor RD. Walk to the RD junction in Stanshope then turn RT and follow the RD to the end of the village, passing Grange Farm (3).

Look for a PF sign at the end of the village, turning LT off the RD. Go through a gate and walk along the top side of the field. Go through an opening in the wall and over several fields on the way to Wetton. Keep generally in the same direction, walking diagonally over the fields.

You come to a minor RD at GR.118547 (4), continue over several fields again towards the pointed hill behind the village of Wetton. Walk for 180m to a PF on the RT. Cross over several more fields emerging on a single track RD and walking into the village of Wetton.

As you get into the centre of Wetton, just before the pub, turn RT and walk up past Town End Farm as you leave the village. At the RD junction just past the farm (5), turn RT between the two RD's and descend the field looking for a gate at the bottom. Go through and follow the path over several fields, slightly bearing RT to Windledale Hollow then on to Brook Lodge (6).

When you reach the minor RD by Brook Lodge, go through the small gate and turn RT, and follow the RD for 60m. Turn LT on a PF and continue over several fields to a 4-way signpost. Walk straight ahead at the sign and continue over a minor RD and over the hillside towards Alstonefield, which you can see ahead.

You come to the sports field in Alstonefield then turn RT onto the RD and LT to take you back to your start point.

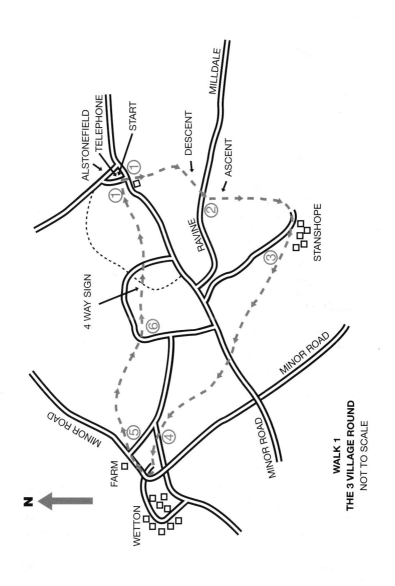

N

ALSTONEFIELD
TELEPHONE
START
①
①
DESCENT
ASCENT
RAVINE
② STANSHOPE
③
4 WAY SIGN
⑥
MINOR ROAD
MINOR ROAD
⑤
④
FARM
WETTON
MINOR ROAD
MILLDALE

WALK 1
THE 3 VILLAGE ROUND
NOT TO SCALE

Walk 2 The Tissington Round   **Distance** 4.5 miles/7.2 km
Start GR. 175524 Park and start from the parking area beside Tissington Hall.
Time 2 hrs
Terrain A nice walk with two ascents, otherwise not too strenuous and good views from the hillsides.

Starting from opposite Tissington Hall, descend the RD past the tearoom and at the green, a short distance further, turn RT, walking past the candle workshop and over a cattle grid. Bear RT 120m past the cattle grid, following the PF sign along by a wall (1). The path leads behind Tissington Hall as you go through a small gate and ascend the field.

Go through another gate as the path bears LT and crosses a stile leading onto the main RD. Cross the RD and stile then go through the opening at the far side, following the PF sign to an opening in the wall at the bottom of the field (2).

Ascend the hillside in front. When halfway up, the path leads into a side field on the LT then continues to the top. When on the flat ground at the top, walk directly to the wall at the far side. Look for the opening through the wall leading to the minor RD.

Cross the RD, and go over a stile to walk on a distinct track winding up the hillside. Turn RT 350m along the track (3) following the PF sign over the wall to Grange. Look for the yellow arrows and ascend diagonally over the fields in the same direction.

As you approach Boston Grange Farm, walk to the RT of it, looking for a step over the stone wall on your RT and ascend towards the mast on the RT (4). Go through a gate at the top and continue over the far side, descending to an access track and the minor RD close by.

Turn RT on the minor RD for 50m and LT soon after following a PF sign through a thin line of trees and cross the field, passing Standlow Farm. Keep the farm to your LT and walk by a wall on a track towards the main RD.

Emerging on the main RD, cross and follow the PF sign along the lane and round to Newton Grange Farm (5). Going round the RT hand bend, a PF sign points across the field on the LT, behind the farm. Follow it diagonally RT as it descends then ascends through openings and over stiles in further fields.

Keeping in the same direction from Newton Grange Farm, you emerge on a minor RD (6) on the outskirts of Tissington. Continue straight along the RD, taking you back into Tissington where you started.

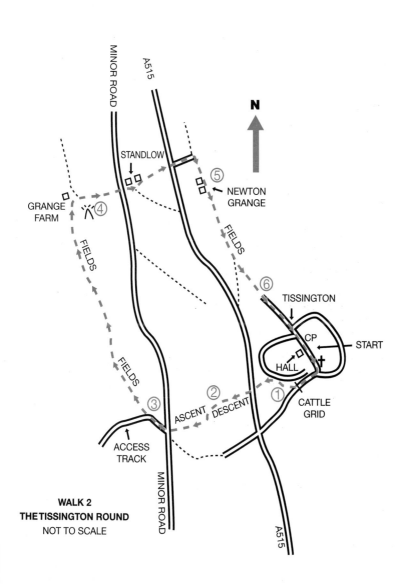

MINOR ROAD

A515

STANDLOW

N

⑤ NEWTON
GRANGE

GRANGE
FARM

⋀ ④

FIELDS

FIELDS

TISSINGTON

⑥

CP

START

HALL

② ① CATTLE
GRID

③ ASCENT DESCENT

FIELDS

ACCESS
TRACK

MINOR ROAD

WALK 2
THE TISSINGTON ROUND
NOT TO SCALE

A515

Walk 3 The Waterwheel Walk   **Distance** 4.7 miles/7.5 km
Start GR. 200436 Beside the pond at the village green in Osmaston
Walk Time 1hr 30 mins
Terrain An excellent walk through woodland and past the scenic lake and waterwheel. A few short and steep ascents/descents, but well worth walking.

Start by following the BW at the end of the row of thatched cottages by the village pond (1), following the Bonnie Prince Charlie walk signs along a track. This track soon passes through woodland and descends to a lake and a waterwheel at the bottom. Keep the waterwheel on your RT as you ascend the path through woodland by the building there to the top on a short steep ascent (2).

At the top of the hillside, keep in a straight line to descend again at the side of woodland, round a barrier and past a house. You come to a narrow RD and continue to descend to Shirley Village. Just as you get to the village, look for a PF sign on your RT and ascend several steps to cross a stile, walking by the RT side of a bungalow (3) then along the side of a field.

Keep the hedge line on your LT and descend the field to the bottom and cross a stile there. Continue descending, over another stile towards woodland. A large house called Shirley House is off to your RT as you walk on the path and cross a field and stiles to the corner of the wood at Shirley Park.

Cross a FB and stile then bear RT, following the worn path through the woodland and over another FB. Keep on the main path, which leads onto a track. You come to a gate as you reach the lake and your path bears LT by the lake and you walk by the lake to a stile at the far end (4). Stay on the worn grass path, ignoring PF on the LT and RT.

Cross several stiles before you come to a slightly boggy area (5). Look for a gate turning sharp RT into the wood. Follow the BW through the wood and ascend the short hillside to go through the fields following the track to a house and access RD there (6).

Follow the access RD, winding LT. This leads round to a wider access RD 400m further. Turn LT here. You should see the church and thatched houses ahead as you walk 300m back to where you originally started.

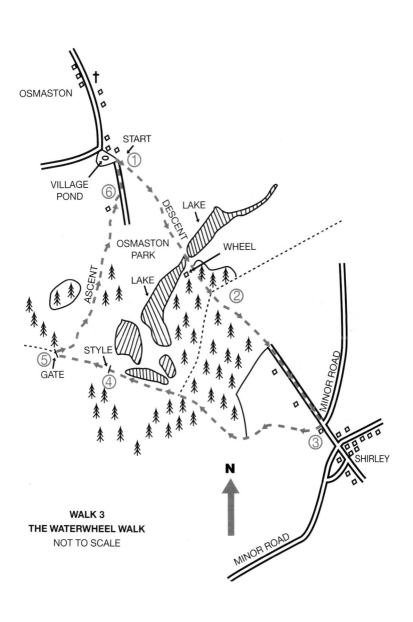

OSMASTON

START

①

VILLAGE
POND

⑥

DESCENT

LAKE

OSMASTON
PARK

WHEEL

ASCENT

LAKE

②

STYLE

④

⑤
GATE

③

MINOR ROAD

SHIRLEY

N

MINOR ROAD

WALK 3
THE WATERWHEEL WALK
NOT TO SCALE

Walk 4 The Manifold Way Circular   **Distance** 5 miles/8 km
Start GR. 100542 Start from Weag's Bridge on The Manifold
Way, 2km from Grindon
Walk Time 2 hrs 15 mins
Terrain A flat walk for the first half then one steep climb to the
RD, and further on a gentle descent back to the river.

From the parking area by Weag's Bridge, walk to the bridge and continue straight along by the sign that states 'cyclists' (1). Keep the river just off to your LT. You come to a caravan park area.

Follow the track as it bears round to the RT (2). Passing the caravans, you come to a bridge, cross and continue on this track for approx. 4km. You come to Lee House tearoom and gardens on your LT (3). Walk past the cottage and over a bridge and as the RD bears LT, look for a FB on your LT, crossing a stream.

This path directly ascends steeply through the wooded area (4) for 900m to emerge at the RD at the top. Turn LT at the RD and walk for 600m towards the entrance to Throwley Cottage by the copse. A PF sign is on your LT pointing across the open field just before the entrance to Throwley Cottage.

Follow the sign across the field, bearing 349°M from the RD. Walk across the field (5), heading towards the RT of woodland along the small ridge before descending into the valley.

Walking for 1.9km from the RD, takes you onto an access track at the bottom of the hillside at the far end. You should see the spire of the church at Grindon on your way.

At the bottom of the hill by the river, the track joins another track, where you turn LT and cross a bridge, soon to follow your original track and the course of the river back to Weag's Bridge, 1.3km further.

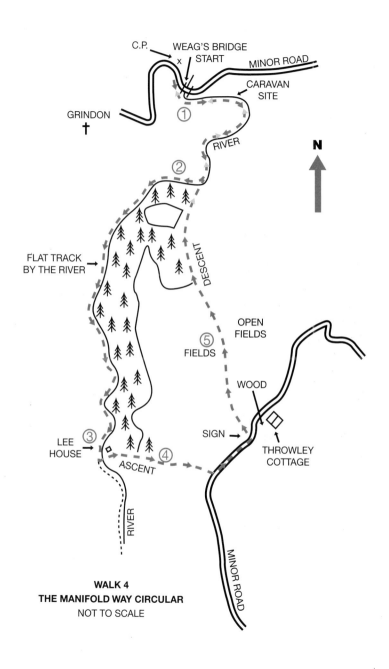

C.P. ← x
WEAG'S BRIDGE
START
MINOR ROAD
CARAVAN SITE
GRINDON †
①
RIVER
N
②
FLAT TRACK BY THE RIVER →
DESCENT
OPEN FIELDS
⑤
FIELDS
WOOD
SIGN →
THROWLEY COTTAGE
LEE HOUSE →
③
④
ASCENT
RIVER
MINOR ROAD

WALK 4
THE MANIFOLD WAY CIRCULAR
NOT TO SCALE

Walk 5 Yerley Hill Round **Distance** 5.3 miles/8.5 km
Start GR. 165480 Park beside The Okeover Arms at Mapleton
Walk Time 2 hrs 10 min
Terrain Mostly flat with only a few ascents/descents. A nice picturesque walk.

Opposite The Okeover Arms pub, cross the RD and go through a small opening into a field. Cross the field diagonally RT to the RD and cross it to the stile opposite. Walking now on a grass path along by the river (1), cross a stile, keeping the river on the LT. Cross several fields then through several kissing gates.

You come to a gate leading into woodland. Go through and stay by the river, crossing several stiles and passing Dove Cottage as you eventually emerge at Coldwall Bridge (2). Go over the stile there then cross the stone bridge to the far side. Go through the gate at the far side and follow the access track as it winds round and ascends the hillside up to Coldwall Farm.

Go through a gate onto the access track by the farm and continue past the farm to the minor RD 100m further. Cross the RD into a field, following the PF sign there which takes you over the brow of the hill towards a farm you should see on the hillside 700m further, which is Woodhouses, and on to the minor RD there at GR.139488 (3).

Emerging on the minor RD, turn LT and walk past Woodhouses. As you come to the small green at the RT of the house, look for a barn close by ahead. Walk to the LT of it and go through a gate onto a distinct track at GR.140487. Continue on this track for 1km on a slight descent then over level ground. Pass an old barn and through gates and over stiles to a house called Martin Hill.

At Martin Hill, walk in front of it then turn LT through a metal farm gate following a yellow arrow near the stables at the far side. Follow the worn grass path, generally in an easterly direction through the fields and over a stiles, keeping the wall to your RT. Continue towards Cowclose Wood you see ahead and cross the field towards the opening between the two parts of the wood (4), at the far side of the field at GR.149479.

You come to a stone wall round the RT side of the wood but continue through the gate between the two parts of the wood and straight on over the field to a ruined house 200m further. Follow the feint grass path and cross a stile by a farm gate as you descend the hillside, keeping Okeover Hall (5) 200m off to your LT.

You come to a minor RD, turning LT there to walk to the RD junction. Turn RT at the junction, walking 210m to the river bridge. Cross the bridge and bear RT just after it, to take you back to your original start point by the Okeover Arms.

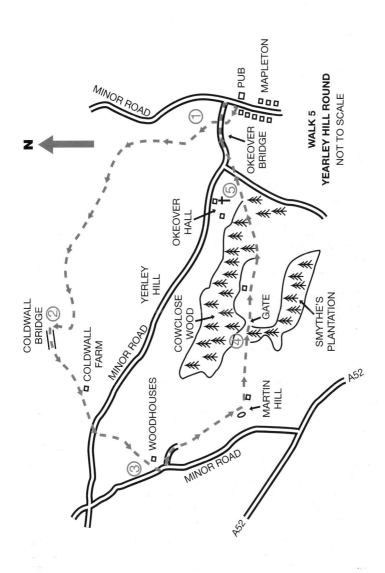

N

MINOR ROAD

PUB

MAPLETON

① OKEOVER BRIDGE

⑤ OKEOVER HALL

YERLEY HILL

MINOR ROAD

COLDWALL BRIDGE ②

COLDWALL FARM

COWCLOSE WOOD

④ GATE

SMYTHE'S PLANTATION

WOODHOUSES

③ MARTIN HILL

MINOR ROAD

A52

A52

WALK 5
YEARLEY HILL ROUND
NOT TO SCALE

Walk 6 The Tissington to Fenny Bentley Trail

Distance 5.3 miles/ 8.6 km

Start GR. 175524 Park and start from the parking area beside Tissington Hall

Walk Time 2 hrs

Terrain Some short hillsides to ascend/descend but overall, a nice walk over fields and a possible refreshment stop at the Dog & Partridge pub in Thorpe!

Leaving from outside the old hall, descend the lane to pass the church on your LT. Turn LT at the bottom and ascend the RD, passing the village pond. The RD bends slightly RT then LT before crossing a cattle grid.

Walk for 100m before turning RT (1) along an access track opposite a farm building. A sign points to Bassett Wood Farm. Walk by the side of a wood on the access track and as you reach a RT hand bend, do not turn RT on the access track, but turn off the access track and through a small opening at the side of a farm gate (2).

Cross the first field then bear slightly RT in the second field and through a farm gate into the next field. Walk for 130m then bear RT towards a small copse. Look for a small gate with a yellow arrow on it. Go through and descend the field through a second small gate nearly to the bottom of the hill. Nearing the bottom, bear RT towards Lees Farm (3).

Follow the path in front of the farm and cross the access track then through a small gate into the field at the far side. Cross several fields to emerge by the old school and telephone in Fenny Bentley. Turn RT on the A515 walking for 20m on the pavement then cross with care into the entrance to the churchyard in Fenny Bentley (4).

Walk along the church path passing the church entrance and continue to the RD at the far side in the village. Turn LT and walk, for 200m passing the houses to the far end. Look for a PF sign on the RT to Thorpe. Turn here and ascend the hillside by a wire fence, going through a gate on the way to the top then cross several fields in the same direction. Go through a gate before descending a hillside diagonally to a small FB over a brook (5).

Ascend the path through the wood emerging on a minor RD. Turn RT and continue on to the Dog and Partridge pub at the top of the lane on the outskirts of Thorpe. Walk round to the RT of it and descend the RD following the sign towards Thorpe.

At the bottom of the hill, cross to the entrance of the Peverill of the Peak

Hotel and cross a stile on the RT, just nearby the entrance (6). Cross a further stile soon after as you now walk on the Limestone Way.

You come to a gate and follow the Tissington sign in the same direction as you ascend the hillside. You emerge on a minor RD. Turn LT for 50m then RT, following a PF sign for Tissington and walking diagonally across several fields to a RD.

Cross the RD and walk in the same direction to the minor RD. Ascend the lane to the junction of the A515. Cross the main RD with care and walk between the stone pillars (7) opposite for 900m back into Tissington.

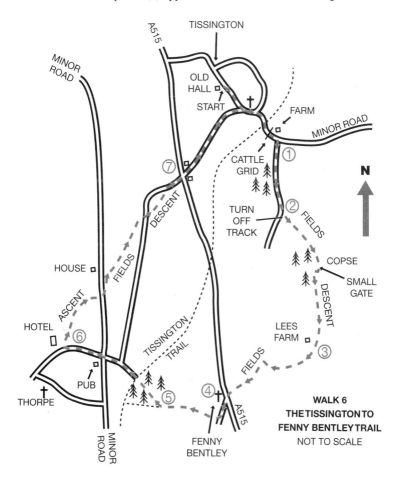

WALK 6
THE TISSINGTON TO
FENNY BENTLEY TRAIL
NOT TO SCALE

Walk 7 Ilam to Calton Round   **Distance** 5.6 miles/9 km
Start GR. 135509 Park in Ilam near the monument
Walk Time 3hrs
Terrain Generally with not much hill climbing. A pleasant walk through the ravine.

Start by the entrance to Ilam Country Park. Stay on the RD and walk around the bend to the school 100m further. Opposite the school turn LT, following the PF sign, cross a stile there and walk along the track (1), keeping the stone wall on your LT. The track crosses Ilam Park.

Continue straight across the field, at the far side, walk parallel with the ridges in the field (2). Look for the FB crossing the river. At the far side, go through a small gate, bearing slightly RT as you head over several fields through gaps in the walls or through small gates towards the farm at Rushley (3).

At Rushley Farm, walk between the barns on the access RD to the far end by the cattle grid. Do not cross it, but turn RT through a gate on your RT then on the grass path into the ravine. Continue on the main path through the ravine to the far end where you may see the village of Calton ahead. Continue over the fields to emerge on the RD near Calton Green (4).

Turn LT on the minor RD for 210m to the RD junction, then LT again for 100m, passing two houses. Look for a PF sign on LT, turn here and walk in front of a farm. Soon you turn LT again, keeping the hedge to your LT. Look for yellow marker post as you cross steps over a wall then walk diagonally across the next field.

You see a house ahead called Fieldhead. Walk in front of it (5) then look for a PF sign. Take the RT hand path and walk in the same general direction around the hillside. Do not cross over the large ladder stile there (6), but continue over the field then over a step to cross the wall. Descend the hillside towards the trees on the hill. Then bear RT towards the minor RD.

Emerging on the RD, turn LT, walk along then after a short ascent, you pass a PF sign on the LT. Do not take that path but continue 140m further. Cross a stile on the LT by this PF sign (7) into a field then soon cross a further stile. Take a bearing from the stile of 41°M and descend the field to the RD at the bottom. Look for a stile over the wire fence onto the RD.

Cross onto the RD then turn LT. You pass a CP and grass area with seats (8). Go through a gate at the far end of the grassed area and walk on the path past the 'Blore Wood' sign and descend towards Ilam.

Your path returns to the RD again. Turn RT on the RD and walk for 500m back into Ilam.

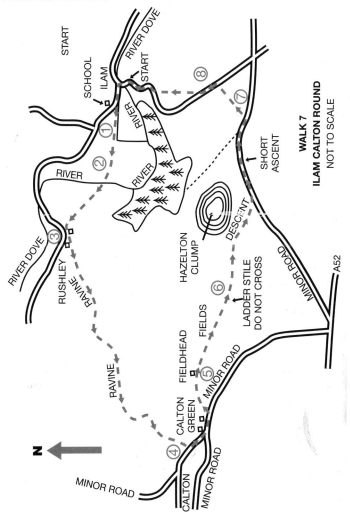

Walk 8 Clifton & Compton Circular   **Distance** 5.9 miles/9.5 km
Start GR. 178463 Outside of Ashbourne Leisure Centre by the mini roundabout on Station St.
Walk Time 3hrs
Terrain A pleasant walk with several short steep sections. A good walk to use your navigation and observation skills

Leaving the roundabout, look for a sign to North Lees on the side of a house about 20m away. Follow it, ascending a narrow path by the LT of some houses then ascending in front of a row of houses (1) to a stile at the top. Emerging in a field, cross it and walk to the top of the field and over a stile by the mast onto the RD.

Turn RT on the RD and continue along Wyaston RD to a roundabout and go straight across then LT along Willow Meadow RD. On reaching Chestnut Drive, turn into it, walking to the bottom of the cul de sac and along a path between the houses. Walk behind the houses and down a flight of steps and over a FB.

Ascend the field (2) and go over two stiles to emerge on the busy A52 RD. Cross the RD with care and ascend the steps on the far side into a caravan site. Walk to the far side of the site on the access RD then turn RT, keeping the hedge line just to your LT. Continue to the far corner of the site to pick up a path through the wood then cross a stile leading out of the wood at the far side at GR. 187449 (3).

Cross a second stile and walk along the edge of the fields in a southwesterly direction, keeping the hedge now on your RT. You see a farm ahead 700m further, nearing it, there is a farm gate just to your RT, with a house at the top of the field. Turn RT there and ascend the field, with the hedge to your LT and walk to the LT of the house to emerge on the minor RD.

Cross a stile at the far side of the RD then cross the field to the far RT corner by a farm (4) then continue past the farm and descend towards the RT side of the wood ahead. You come to a farm gate by the wood leading into a large field. Walk across the field, looking for a small stone post and narrow opening concealed in the hedge line directly across (see sketch).

Go through the opening and walk to the far side of the field as you descend towards a farm below, walking to the RT of a small wood. At the bottom, walk to a copse ahead then just before it, turn RT to ascend the hillside (5) to a stile at the top LT, heading towards a golf course. Walk along the edge of the field for 20m then turn RT onto the golf course.

Following yellow arrows, walk west, straight down the golf course to the main A517 RD (6). The minor RD into Clifton Village is opposite. Cross with care and follow the RD through the village of Clifton, turning RT on a minor RD just past The Cock Inn pub. Follow the lane called Watery Lane to the junction of the A52 (7) then turn LT walking to Hanging Bridge.

At a hotel on the RT called The Royal Oak, turn RT to walk along the far side of it and where the lane winds round, continue in same direction through several fields and along by the River Dove. The path bears RT away from the river along an embankment. Approaching a farm (8), the path bears diagonally LT. Follow it towards a hill you should see ahead.

As you ascend the hillside, you come to a short track and a farm gate at GR. 169464. Ashbourne is just on the far side of the hill now. Go through the farm gate and follow the track as it winds over the hillside towards a small wood on the top (9). Go over two stiles and follow the access track down to the main RD through Ashbourne.

The main Parish Church of St Oswald is nearby. Walk past the church then turn RT at the next main RD to arrive back at the mini roundabout by the sports centre.

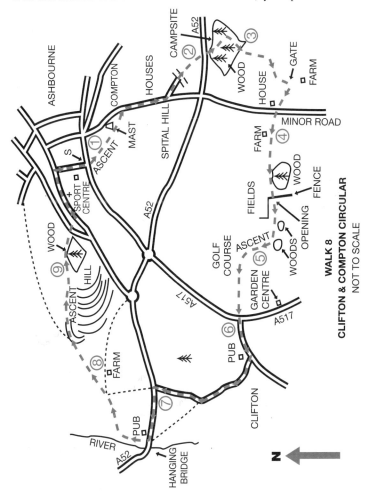

WALK 8
CLIFTON & COMPTON CIRCULAR
NOT TO SCALE

Walk 9 Dove Dale, Wood & River Walk   **Distance** 7 miles/11.3 km
Start GR. 147509 Start from the Nat. Trust CP just past the Izaak Walton
Hotel at the entrance to Dovedale
Walk Time 3hrs
Terrain An excellent mainly flat scenic walk through Dove Dale and Hall Dale
with two short climbs out of Hall Dale and over Bunster Hill near the end.

Leaving the CP, walk to the RT of the toilets (1) along the path, keeping the river on
your RT. When you come to the signboards by the FB, walk straight ahead to cross
the stepping stones further on. If the stepping stones are submerged, (a sign there
will say so) then cross the FB and walk along the RT side of the river.

Arriving at the stepping stones over the river, cross to the RT side and continue on
the path with the river on your LT now. You ascend then descend some steps on
the path before coming to another FB further on, with a large rock called Ilam Rock
on the far side of the FB (2).

Cross the FB and walk on the LT side of the river now. Follow the sign there to
Stanshope. You come to an opening in a wall and another sign 450m further. Turn
LT there along Hall Dale (ravine) towards Stanshope and continue until eventually
you come to a stone wall across your path with a wooden gate and sign for Hall
Dale near the far end.

Go through the gate then soon after is another wall across the path. You should see
the village of Stanshope ahead. Look on your LT for an opening in the wall (3) and
go through to ascend a short steep hillside, keeping the stone wall on your RT as
you ascend. Cross a stile at the top and continue close by the wall to the far end of
the field. Look for a barn on the hillside to your RT, which you will soon pass.

You come to an old mine entrance. Look for the posts with yellow arrow and walk
to the RT of the mine on the higher ground and onto an old track through two farm
gates. The track turns RT between two walls towards the barn on higher ground.

When you reach the barn (4), go through a gate at the far side on your RT then bear
LT to go through another farm gate into the next field. Walk to the far LT corner of
that field and go through a small gate to emerge on a minor RD. Turn LT on the RD
and walk for 1km, descending the RD.

Where the RD bends RT, cross a cattle grid on your LT (5) onto an access track
then take a bearing of 160°M and cross the field to ascend the ridge (6) and walk
over Bunster Hill. Keep in the same general direction as you descend the other side,
looking for the worn grass path, do not continue on the high ground to the LT.

While descending, look for the large hotel (7) 600m across two fields in the same
direction. Cross stiles and through gates to pass the LT side of the hotel. At the far
side of the hotel, take the LT path back to the CP 230m further.

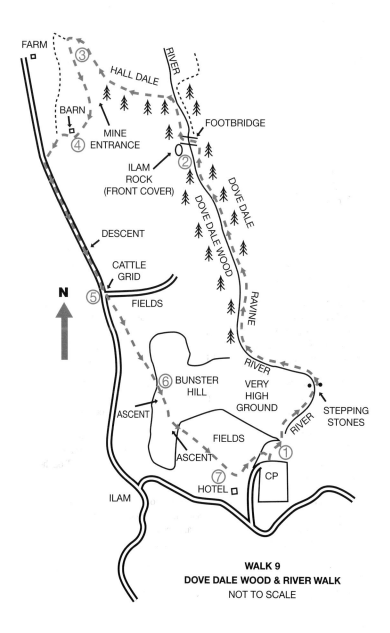

FARM

③ HALL DALE

RIVER

BARN

④ MINE ENTRANCE

FOOTBRIDGE

ILAM ROCK (FRONT COVER)

②

DOVE DALE

DESCENT

DOVE DALE WOOD

CATTLE GRID

N

⑤ FIELDS

RAVINE

RIVER

⑥ BUNSTER HILL

VERY HIGH GROUND

STEPPING STONES

ASCENT

FIELDS

RIVER

①

ASCENT

⑦ HOTEL

CP

ILAM

WALK 9
DOVE DALE WOOD & RIVER WALK
NOT TO SCALE

Notes